# Abinadi and King Noah

written by Tiffany Thomas
illustrated by Nikki Casassa

CFI · An imprint of Cedar Fort, Inc. · Springville, Utah

## HARD WORDS:
Abinadi, Noah, baptize

## PARENT TIP: At the end of the story, have your child act out what was read.

This is Abinadi.
Abinadi is a
man of God.

This is King Noah.
King Noah is very bad.

Abinadi tells the people
King Noah is bad.

The people get mad.
King Noah is mad, too.

Alma hears Abinadi.

Alma runs away
from King Noah.

King Noah kills Abinadi with fire.

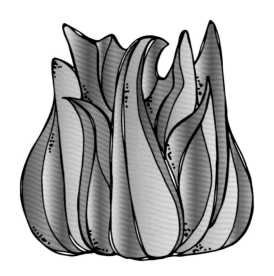

Alma tells the people what Abinadi said.

9

The good people are baptized.

King Noah is mad.
God tells Alma and
his people to run away.

11

They find
King Mosiah
and are safe.

The end.

ISBN 13: 978-1-4621-4337-5

Published by CFI, an imprint of Cedar Fort, Inc. • 2373 W. 700 S., Suite 100, Springville, UT 84663
Distributed by Cedar Fort, Inc., www.cedarfort.com

Cover design and interior layout design by Shawnda T. Craig
Cover design © 2022 Cedar Fort, Inc.
Printed in China • Printed on acid-free paper
10 9 8 7 6 5 4 3 2 1